Princes Risborough
in old picture postcards

by
A.J. Macfarlane

Monks Risborough 1996.

*With very best wishes to
Desmond & Caroline.
from John Rivett
Burton Lane MR.*

European Library – Zaltbommel/Netherlands

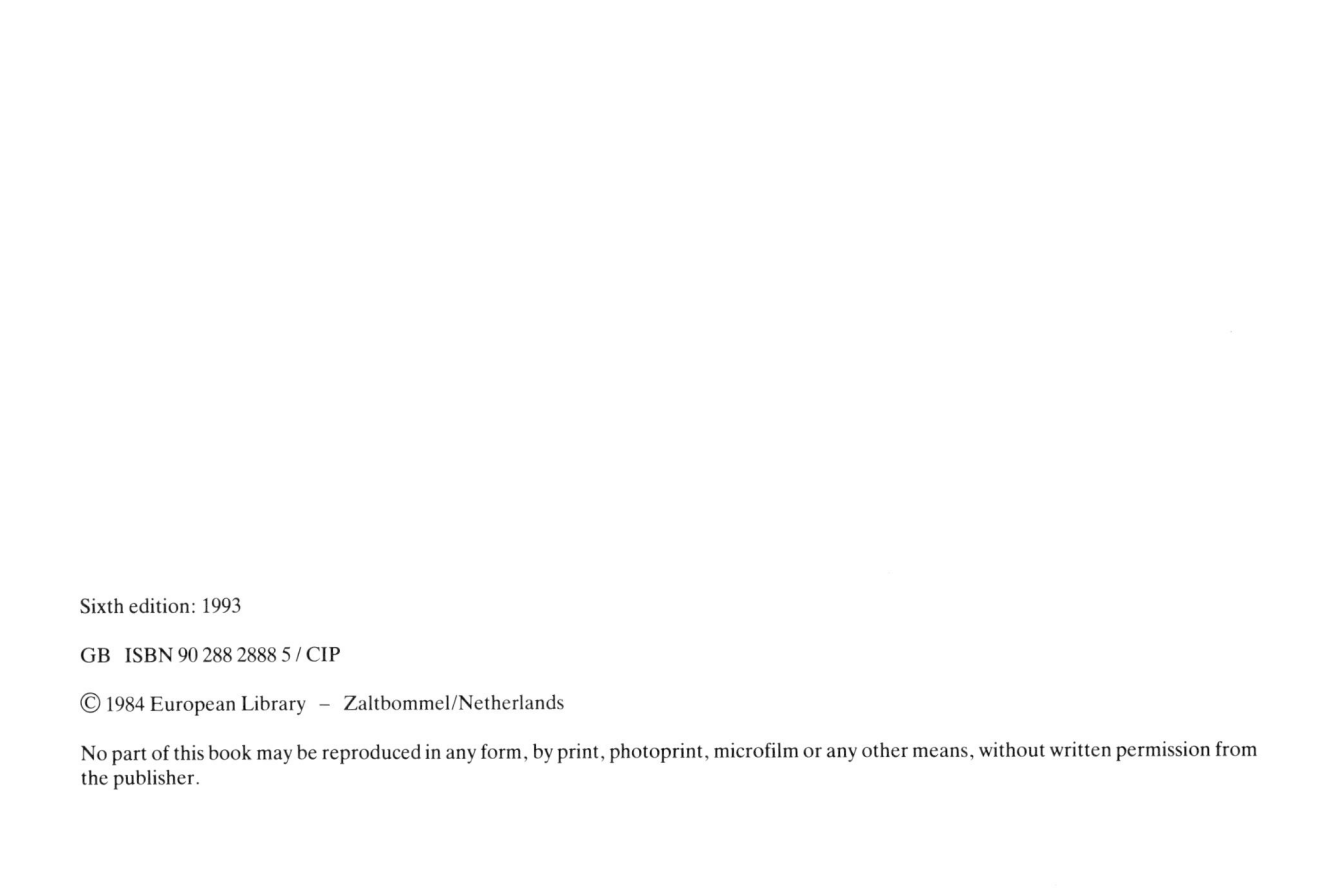

Acknowledgement:
My special thanks to Mrs. Janet Foster for the help in preparing the typescript.

Sixth edition: 1993

GB   ISBN 90 288 2888 5 / CIP

© 1984 European Library – Zaltbommel/Netherlands

No part of this book may be reproduced in any form, by print, photoprint, microfilm or any other means, without written permission from the publisher.

INTRODUCTION

Although this collection of pictures is intended to give an idea of what it was like to live in Princes Risborough in the fifty years from 1880-1930, the area has been of some importance from earliest times and a little of its history may not be out of place, though those interested will find several more scholarly works at their disposal.

The town lies in a broad gap in the western slopes of the Chiltern Hills, as they look out over the Vale of Aylesbury, between the ancient Upper Icknield Way to the South and the more probably Roman Lower Icknield Way to the North. The chalk-cut Whiteleaf Cross overlooks it, beside which, and on the other side of the gap, are Neolithic and Bronze Age mounds. Indeed, in recent months a Bronze Age burial has been uncovered within the town itself. On Pulpit Hill to the east are the remains of an Iron Age hill fort, and a Romano-British villa lay in the valley at Saunderton. The Domesday Book records that 'Riseberge' was a village of Earl Harold, last Saxon King of England, and it eventually passed into the keeping of Edward, the Black Prince, from whom its present name is said to be derived. Earthworks west of St. Mary's Church, often referred to as Saxon, are traditionally associated with him, though the only records definitely linking the Black Prince with the manor relate not to residence but to his stud farm. Henry VIII granted rights to a market and two fairs, on 'the eve, day and morrow' of the Nativity of the Virgin Mary, and of the escape from martyrdom of St. George, and, although the days have changed, the fairs are still held, centred on 6th May and 21st October. Elizabeth I issued letters reciting various grants made by herself and her ancestors to the townsfolk, which are loosely referred to as the 'Risborough Charter' and are perhaps most interesting for the family names mentioned and which can still be met with in the town today.

In 1861, Sheahan described *a small, neat Market town, consisting of one principal street, and smaller ones diverging,* the nucleus of the town as it is today. As our story opens, the population was about 2,500 in the Parish with some 550 inhabited houses in the town, a population figure which had increased by about 500 since the coming of the railway, but remained fairly static for the next fifty years. Kelly's Directory of 1883 shows the community to have been remarkably self-sufficient. The railway was firmly established, and by 1900 there were five trains a day to Watlington, five to Oxford, with an extra on Tuesdays for Thame market, and a regular service to London, taking one hour and ten minutes for the journey. The Gaslight and Coke Company had opened in 1863, the streets having previously been lit by Camphine, a kind of turpentine. Water came from springs and although in 1926 the first main water supply was installed, at half cost price to the first hundred takers, at least one old well remained in regular use until the 1970's. Every item of clothing could be made and bought in the town, from Joseph Castle's boots and shoes to the Misses Barnard's millinery. There were two doctors, a chemist and medical herbalist, not to mention the Inspector of Public Nuisances. Lace making and chair turning, two traditional Buckinghamshire cottage industries. were still well represented. The brewery was backed up by no less than eleven hotels and inns, and three beer retailers, though it should be said that many of these carried only intermittent trade. There was a strong community spirit, witnessed in Press reports of such great occasions of the period as Queen Victoria's Jubilee in 1897, the celebration of the relief of Mafeking in 1900, when at 24 hours notice a parade was organised of floats and 53 cyclists 'in costume, led by Doctors McKay and Watson on horseback', and the Coronation of King George V when 'the whole of the householders decorated the streets with bunting, flags and fairy lights, the brewery donated an 18 gallon cask of best beer, and 400 people at a time sat down to eat in the great Malthouse hall.' Of course, life was not all 'beer and skittles'; the weather was not always as kind as old pictures would have us believe, for one thing. In 1881 a two day fall of snow buried a train of seven coaches at Saunderton up to its wheels, and trapped the relief train sent to rescue it, and in 1895 the Thames froze over at Marlow. There were even earthquakes in 1887 and 1889! The Great War took its toll, and whilst cholera might have been a thing of the past other infectious illnesses were a very real threat, and an outbreak of measles would close a school immediately. Nevertheless there was a sense of order in a town that had not changed much in a century.

I hope that these pictures, which have for the most part been placed at my disposal by generous friends, will both refresh the memories of those who have seen Prince's Risborough change (and lose its apostrophe!), and stimulate an interest and affection in those who, like myself, have only known it in modern guise. Scarcely a month goes by without some feature changing or disappearing, and it takes a brave man to stand in the road today and repeat the views that were taken up to a hundred years ago, when the car from Chequers Court could be heard while still a quarter of a mile distant. Yet the traces of the past are still there, to show how Princes Risborough was, to paraphrase J.H.B. Peel, 'hub of this small universe, that spins the better for it.'

Sources of Pictures:
Mrs. M. Bedford: 5
Terry Brisco: 63
Mrs. Brock: 73
Mrs. D. Burridge: 76
Miss East: 71
Miss Janes: 18, 42, 62, 75
Mr. J. Milton: 12, 20, 38
Mr. J. Newitt: 1, 8, 33, 35, 36, 37, 41, 64
Mr. D. Parker: 4, 6, 7, 9, 15, 16, 21, 25, 30, 34, 39, 43, 48, 49, 54, 59
Mr. H. Percival: 10
Mr. & Mrs. C. Poulton: 66, 67, 72
Mr. F. Spittles: 40, 46, 47, 50, 51, 55, 58, 60
Miss A. Stratton: 17, 29, 45
Mrs. B.M. Wallen: 57
Mr. & Mrs. Williams: 65, 69, 70, 74
Mr. L. Wright: 52
All other pictures are the property of the author.

PRINCES RISBOROUGH, FROM WHITE LEAF CROSS.   TAUNT & CO. 1503

1. Let us start our journey through the town with a bird's eye view from Kop Hill, taken about 1900. The detail of the town may be difficult to discern, but the Brewery chimney and malthouse mark the centre beyond the trees of Little Park, and the white line of the Wycombe Road can be seen pointing to Bledlow Cop. At the time of the Inclosures the dark fields in the middle ground formed one large area known as Burying Field, now built over, with smaller named 'Pieces' such as Quilter's and Swinner's, roughly where The Crescent now stands. The footpath crossing the fields on the right, which now runs between Berryfield and Woodfield Roads, leaving the town at Crossfield Road, was the main route to Whiteleaf, and the field it crosses was saved from threat of development in 1935, when such men as John Nash, the artist, and F.G. Parsons, local historian, wrote to The Times appealing for help to preserve 'the finest view in the South of England', and raised £3,000 to place it in the hands of the National Trust. Little did they guess what lay only fifteen years ahead, and how grateful we should be for their foresight.

2. This was the view in 1880 from Ward's Park (now Wade's Field), looking across Bull Close, where the bonfires burned on Mafeking night, to the Parish Church and Chiltern escarpment. We shall return for a closer look at the church and its old spire, but note the little turret of the malthouse just showing behind the eastern end. Monks Staithe, on the left, is unchanged today; by repute the home of monks from Notley Abbey, it is perhaps as famous for its spiders! A striking feature of this view is the broad cultivation of the slopes leading to Kop Hill, traces of which can still be seen today, though scrub now covers the hillside as it also encloses Whiteleaf Cross, recalling the old description of the town 'Hrisebyrgan be Cilternes efese — the brush-covered hills by the Chiltern eaves'.

3. This view is taken from what is now the corner of The Avenue and Aylesbury Road, showing the only houses in Queen's Road — Chiltern Retreat or Clovellie as it was called then, and the row of cottages grandly named Chiltern College on the 1880 Ordnance Survey map. The small triangle of roof in the garden of Clovellie marks a little gem of Victorian architecture, a goat house! Where the corn stood in front of the cottages, the Church of England 'Waifs and Strays Girls Home', now St. Agatha's Children's Home, was erected in 1907 by his widow as a memorial to the Reverend R. Bardolph, Rector of Princes Risborough. The opening was a great occasion, attended by the Lord Mayor of London.

4. The approach to the town remained virtually undeveloped until after 1930, though the motor car was certainly making its presence felt, both for itself and in related advertising! The country verges were soon to disappear, though Wellington Farm remained as agricultural land until the 1960's apart from the field on the right. This was presented to the children as the first King George V Playing Field in the country, in response to the King's Jubilee Appeal, by Mr. E.J. Turner, J.P., who lived at The Chilterns opposite. It saved his view, but was a generous gift which now provides almost the only green space left within the town.

5. This delightful picture epitomises the rural life that this book seeks to recapture. This pair of cottages was the home of the Goodchild and Janes families; the Great War is not long over and Mr. Goodchild, still in uniform, is seen here with his family and friends. Beside him his wife holds their daughter, Minnie, now Mrs. Bedford, who lent me this family treasure. Mr. Goodchild had been a drayman for the Brewery before the war and afterwards was a paperhanger for Mr. Lacey of Duke Street. An excellent workman, the story is told of him that he was sent to paper Mr. Turner's front room, the work being satisfactorily completed in the absence of Mr. Turner himself, save for a disagreement about which was the front of the house! The suave young man in the trilby is thought to be the local 'ace' reporter, perhaps the Mr. A. Buccini, from the Buckinghamshire Advertiser, who had a reputation for organising highly successful social gatherings, both in the Chalfont Hall (q.v.) and later at the Whitecross Hall in Monks Risborough. How could this cheerful group, rejoicing in the end of the War to end wars, have dreamed that their own particular bit of England was to survive less than twenty years?

6. I have included this second view of the cottages to give a clearer idea of their overall appearance and their position at the foot of the Aylesbury Road hill, and because it includes a detail of the so-called 'Iron Chapel', home of the Free Baptists during the twenty year period of separation within the town's Baptist congregation from 1870-1890. The land was given by Thomas Parsons, the brewer, who had been a prime mover in the schism, and when no longer required as a Church, the building reverted to the brewery and was commonly known as the Chalfont Hall, since lettings were in the hands of William Chalfont at the Buckingham Arms opposite. The cottages were demolished in 1937 to make way for the new Roman Catholic Church of St. Teresa of Lisieux, and the hall was renamed the Walsingham Hall.

7. The old Buckingham Arms marked the boundary of this end of the town, and standing as it did right beside the road it effectively closed off the view from the Market Square until it was demolished in 1938. It was the stronghold of the Aylesbury Brewery Company at the take-over of the Risborough Brewery, and was managed by Mr. Chalfont, a man of considerable proportions, as a later picture in the book will testify. Some of the old foundations were recently briefly uncovered, during preparatory work for the new relief road, with a suggestion of substantial cellars. Behind it were watercress beds and beyond, down the Thame Road, was the Gasworks. Although improved early in the nineteenth century it is of interest to note that this Thame Road, traces of which can be seen on the right of the present road bridge at Alscot, was described by St. John Priest in his Agricultural Review of 1810 as one which 'no wise man would travel without a guide'.

Duke Street, Princes Risborough.

8. Duke Street was a thriving market street, and somehow its proportions seemed 'right' in 1910. Elaborate shop fronts were in evidence on the right, but on the left as many businesses were carried on behind ordinary front doors. In a relatively closed community there was not the same need as there is today for the public display of goods. On the left was Henry Nottingham's shoe shop and 'Fancy Goods Repository' and on the right the elegant display of Bloss and Sons, here hidden behind its vast sunblind, surmounted by a magnificent wrought-iron grille. Was the sun really so much brighter in those days? Bloss's sold 'a choice variety of locally made pillow lace' and 'our speciality, 30/- suits made-to-measure'. When I first knew it, Duke Street started its house numbering on the left at No. 91 — a street of character!

9. The passage of time has somewhat reduced Duke Street, which now ends on the right, one door beyond the nearest white cottage, and on the left has lost the 'Blue Kettle' with its bay window. Pigot's Directory of 1835 refers to the street as Honey Lane, but by 1842 half the residents describe themselves as being in Duke Street. This was perhaps in deference to the Duke of Wellington after whom Wellington Farm in the background may also have been named, being formerly called Home Farm. The Census of 1881 refers to the street as Crown Lane, and maybe we see here Thomas Busby, landlord of 'The Crown' and also a plumber and glazier, in keeping with the common practice amongst landlords of following a second occupation, their premises perhaps only being used to the full on Market Days. Dickie Jacobs was until recently a familiar face at the second door beyond, he and his father having worked the Smithy just round the corner adjoining Back Lane. In the background the old Buckingham Arms faces squarely up to the town.

10. The distinguished Oxford photographer, Henry Taunt, was a life-long friend of Samuel Adcock the younger, and in addition to his series of views of Risborough, he had the habit of sending his friend a birthday card each year, normally of an unusual milestone with the age substituted for the distance. On this occasion he celebrated fifty years of friendship with a reminder of two partnerships, Adcock and Son as grocers and Taunt and SUN making pictures. Amongst the wares on display are three neatly wrapped sugar loaves by the window and a boar's head on the churn. The sign in the window declares this to be the Post Office. Next door was Solomon Tapping's butchers shop and beyond it White's ironmongery and builders merchants, later continuing in the same business as Lacey's and J.B. Kibble. Compare the thatched cottages in the background with the same cottages in the preceding but later views.

11. This picture appeared in Taunt's guide to 'Risborough and round it' as an advertisement for 'the old-established business where you can get... the greater part of your needs.' The display of goods would do credit to any modern superstore, even down to a tin of Macfarlane Lang's biscuits on top of the stack in the doorway! The folded-away sunblind was a recent innovation, though Bloss and Sons had boasted one for some years. Adcocks later expanded to take over the whole frontage and remained an important feature of the town until 1979 and the retirement of Mr. Harold Percival, nephew of 'the young Samuel Adcock' and seen here as a visitor from London with his sister. Amongst many contributions to the town Mr. Percival numbered founder membership of the Tennis Club.

12. The Market Square in 1890. The uncluttered lines of the Market house with its ladder to the upper floor date back to 1824, when it was restored by John Grubb as a cornmarket, with a clock in the cupola, striking the hours, raised by public subscription. This clock signalled the start of many public events, but was eventually silenced at the request of the inhabitants of the Square. The Wheatsheaf was a Commercial Hotel of considerable repute, run by William Sulston. The pavement on the left was typical, a central brick path with cobbles either side, and traces still show themselves occasionally today. The Gables, in the left background, merits its own picture.

13. An older view of the Gables hangs in the Library, showing it rendered over, when Abel Rogers, Churchwarden and maltster, lived there. Here the plaster has been stripped off to show the full glory of the herring-bone brickwork infilling the square timber framing. Today only the high gables and the massive chimney hint at what lies behind the modern brick facade. I wonder if Mr. Harris, who also ran waggonette trips to local beauty spots, looked back as we are doing now, to a business that flourished over sixty years before his time, when Martha East spun ropes and twine and made fine saddles on these same premises? Next door a notice in the window and two above it remind the passer-by that the Post Office had moved here briefly, before moving into the High Street.

14. Twenty years later and the front of the Gables is once again rendered over. The Wheatsheaf has become the Capital and Counties Bank, which had formerly done business in the High Street. Five business-like windows and an ornate porch mark the new importance of the building. Telegraph poles have begun to clutter the skyline, and the governess cart and horse and cart are overshadowed by the road sign, forerunner of the multiplicity to come now the age of the motor car had arrived. As the Parish Councillors may feel safer for the enclosed staircase which replaced the old ladder giving access to the upper chamber of the Market House, might we not all feel safer if ten miles an hour was still the speed limit in the High Street?

THE MARKET PLACE, PRINCES RISBOROUGH, BUCKS.

15. The Brewery was an important feature of the town for most of the nineteenth century and first quarter of the twentieth century. As the Lion Steam Brewery it was owned by Thomas Parsons; in 1900 the Welch Ale Brewery took it over and in 1920 the Aylesbury Brewery Company acquired it, eventually closing it down in 1927. Thomas Parsons was a man with a finger in many pies; Sun Fire Assurance agent and Collector of Taxes, his machinations within the Baptist congregation have already been mentioned, and he also started the development of Whiteleaf village. The brewery was demolished in 1927 and with it the oast-house, part of the complex between the square and the Manor House. The malthouse hall was taken over by Cheverton and Laidler's paperware factory and is likely to disappear soon as the whole site is redeveloped. The brewery arch survived until 1960, surmounted by a terracotta lion, whose head may just be seen rising out of the foliage and reputedly harboured a swarm of bees. Below the lion a small round hole was just the right size to hold a small barrel of beer on festive occasions. To the right of the arch Friars Cottage still survives, converted into shops. It was the home of Dr. Alfred Wills, who did his rounds on a motor cycle, and later Mr. Redway lived there until moving to Monks Risborough and taking the name of his old home with him.

16. On the right, the beautiful house which is now combined business premises was for many years associated with the Vocations in the town, first as the home of Richard Meade, Perpetual Curate, whose Parish Registers are a rich source of information, and later the home of Dr. Warren, Public Vaccinator. A reminder that all was not serene in the nineteenth century, and a link between the two men, is the Reverend Meade's record of three deaths from smallpox in the 1850's. Amelia Goodchild, aged 26, was buried at midnight, and two others at 10 p.m., to minimise contagion. In 1913 Dr. Francis William Cooper, the first of the modern generation of doctors in the town, lived and held surgeries here. Dr. Cooper was followed in the profession by his son and between them they gave nearly seventy years of service to the town. On the opposite side of the square was Horace Ridley's shop – chemist, stationer and wine merchant. These premises changed hands a great deal and were at one time part of the Bloss holding in the town. In 1979 the shop front was bricked-up and Risborough's newest licensed premises, the Whiteleaf Cross, was opened. In the background of this picture, just covering the angle between roof and wall of Vine House, the keen-eyed may discern the sign of The Star, where Joseph Wooster was retailing beer in 1880.

17. These cottages in Church Street have been a landmark of old Princes Risborough since the time of Henry VI, said a local paper in 1934, when the Sanitary Committee of Wycombe District Council proposed that they be demolished, and were supported in this by virtually all the local representatives. Councillor Major T.M. McGown drew attention to the wish of the owner, Mr. F.H. Parrott, to preserve them after the Council for the Protection of Rural England had suggested turning them into showrooms, and fortunately his amendment was carried by the narrowest of margins. Although the further cottages were demolished, as others round the corner had been many years before to make way for the malthouse, the rest were saved and converted into the Parrott Hall, which at one time housed the Fire Brigade and later the County Library. Plans for a new library in Bell Street leave the future of the hall undecided once again, but one hopes the lesson has been learnt.

18. There were several 'cottage industries' in Princes Risborough, and in Church Street could be found parchment, straw hat and dressmakers, and of course makers of the renowned Buckinghamshire lace. What more appropriate than a picture of Mrs. Sarah Lacey, whose descendants down to great-great-grandchildren are still living in the town? Mrs. Lacey is seen at the age of ninety, with her bolster pillow and characteristic South Buckinghamshire bobbins, in the yard of her home, the farthest of the Tudor cottages just seen, and demolished in 1934. It was probably her husband's grandfather, living in the same cottage in 1820, who, canvassed for his opinion about the proposed Inclosure, wisely replied: 'I serve two masters and shall say nothing, for I shall surely offend one!'

19. Further down Church End was the Rising Sun. George West was the landlord in 1880, and may be pictured here with his family. He was succeeded by Herbert Hickman who, when the Rising Sun eventually closed, opened in its place the Sunset Carriers business. Through the gates in the background were livery stables. Behind the Rising Sun was the first home of the Fire Brigade and subsequently Timothy East's coal yard. No doubt in years to come the thriving Garden Centre of recent years which made this corner of the town once again a meeting point, will be remembered with equal nostalgia. It is perhaps difficult at first sight to believe that the other house shown, tumbledown and with its little cap of thatch, could be the same house as the Corner Cottage of today. Much earlier it had been the cottage of the overseer of the Workhouse, which stood behind it, opposite the Church, and where the Parish registers record that in 1816 'Henry, called Sinful, a traveller' died.

20. Princes Risborough Volunteer Fire Brigade was led by Captain George Stratton for 36 years from its formation in 1870, and subsequently by Henry Nottingham. The Brigade are shown here in 1883 with their new lightweight machine which provoked the envy of their rivals in the many contests that they won. In their dress uniforms of blue tunics trimmed with scarlet braid, and white breeches, they must have cut quite a dash when they won the first prize at the Alexandra Palace in competition with the London Fire Brigade and others. The Brigade did not achieve a motor engine until after 1930, but were nevertheless able to achieve such results as being in action by Bledlow paper mills at 2.10 a.m. 'after receipt of an alarm by mounted messenger at 1.30 a.m.' It is sad to record that despite such an efficient response the cottages of the Beasley, Gomm and Cobb families were lost, but the fault lay, not with the Brigade, but in their isolation and primitive construction, including thatch.

21. The Manor House itself is little changed today, save for the addition of more gable windows to the front and left hand end. The building is a farmhouse dating from the seventeenth century replacing as Manor House a former, separate building 'adorned with rude Caryatides' which had been visited by Elizabeth I. Originally cottages extended from Church Street right round to the Manor House, owned by one William Martin of Great Hampden, who was allotted land in Parkfield in lieu at the Inclosure, and after whom the writer's house is named. The cottages were cleared to make way for Thomas Parsons' malthouse. The Manor House was presented to the National Trust in 1925 by the widow and family of the Honourable Charles Rothschild, and is chiefly known for its magnificent Jacobean staircase.

22. The Parish Church of St. Mary was founded in Norman times, substantially altered in the thirteenth century with a tower added in the fourteenth century. In 1550 'a chalice, a sensure and xj pyxes of sylver' were sold by consent of the whole parish for covering the Church and in 1552 five great bells were hung. In 1803 the old spire fell down, extensively damaging the roof and destroying the peal of bells. The clock was spared; on its movement a brass plate declares: 'Risborough clock I be, Tomlinson of Thame made me in 1783'. The spire shown here was the replacement, and two bells were rehung, one dated 1805 and the other 1861, cast by John Warner of London, in memory of Lovegrove Norris, a surgeon in the town.

23. In 1907 The People reported that *what is regarded as the most unsightly Church spire in England exists at Princes Risborough*. This stone spire, 100 feet high, had been clad in iron and *for many years has presented an indescribably rusty appearance.* Accordingly it was pulled down and replaced by the spire here being 'topped out'. The new tower had no place for Tomlinson's clock, which sits forlornly in the belfry, perhaps because the Market House clock had supplanted it. In 1904 the Monks Risborough Parish Magazine records the contribution to the Fund for the spire of £14 from a provision stall run by ladies of the parish. Such stalls were a major source of revenue to the Spire fund, enthusiastically encouraged by the Rector's daughter, and led to its being referred to uncharitably as 'the Pork Pie and Marmalade Spire'.

Princes' Risborough, Church from the field.   R. Adams. 2470

24. J.O. Scott's new spire is seen to advantage from the path which is now Manor Park Avenue. Originally the main path to the railway station, which as was usual had been built well clear of the town, it ran between Rosewood and Winterfold, seen here. Rosewood on the left backed directly onto Court Close, a field enclosing old earthworks which, as mentioned earlier, were said to be the remains of the Black Prince's palace. Excavations by F.H. Pavry and others suggest it to be one of the largest manorial sites known of this period, remains of an extensive range of buildings of flint and chalk, and paving tiles from Penn being uncovered. These date from about a hundred years before the Black Prince's day, and there were signs of occupation until the seventeenth century. The area was generally known as The Butts. Court Close became known as The Mount and was levelled as allotments and eventually car park. Opposite the entrance the Churchyard fence climbs over all that remains of the earthworks and the name Court Close has been transferred to a nearby modern cul-de-sac.

St. Mary's Church & High Street, Princes Risboro'.

From the Air.

25. Before continuing our journey through the town let us look back at what we have seen so far, but from the air. In the left background is the little spire of the 'Iron Chapel' with the cottages in front of it. On the nearside of Back Lane the white building marks the Smithy. In the centre of the picture is the vast hall of the malthouse with its oast house tower; behind it is the tall, narrow Brewer's house, like a harbourmaster's, overseeing the square, and behind that again the Brewery yard and chimney. In the foreground, below the Church, are the earthworks of The Mount, and on the left the Manor Farm, whose character has been well preserved in the modern houses which have replaced it. In the right middle distance, like a cluster of beach huts, are the ricks of Town Farm and beyond them near the High Street the buildings of Ayres' Farm. Apart from the outlying Parkfield, almost the whole of the old town is shown.

26. In this general view looking up the High Street in about 1905 one's eye is caught by the magnificent chestnut tree outside 'The Yews' and the open fields on the hillside above the White Lion. The George and Dragon on the left had seen the last coach from London via Amersham in 1898. The Post Office on the right delivered mail twice and despatched it five times daily, once on Sundays, through Tring and later Wendover. Postcards were sent for ½d. inland and 1d. overseas, and at a time when there were still single digit telephone numbers in Princes Risborough were a major means of communication, and could deliver a message within a day. The archway just further up the street was in those days the entrance to Ayres' Farm.

27. This photograph was taken by John Hickman, agent for the Prudential Life and Nottinghamshire and Midland Fire Offices, It is not, as one might suppose, a nineteenth century traffic warden about to do his duty; who would have dared to question the propriety of Aunt Ayres parking outside the front door of Ayres' Farm in the High Street, where the premises of Hester-Clark and Charrington's are today? Of the five farmhouses in the town itself only Town Farm in Church Street remained active until the second half of this century, under the care of the Woods family, bringing in the cows for milking regardless of 'the roar of Risboro' traffic'!

28. Here is another view of the High Street, in 1926. The fine house on the left had been the home of Dr. Watson, whose renowned collection of Napoleonic furniture overflowed from the house into a series of outbuildings in the garden. Barclays Bank now occupies the building, also swallowing up the little office of Gossling and Redway, where much of the development talked of in this book was handled, Hamnett Raffety not opening a local office until 1951. Gossling and Redway moved across the street to the premises now occupied by their successors, Vernon and Son. The sunblind shades the High Class Butcher's shop of George Lacey, whom we shall see later. The striped pole indicates the 'Haircutting and Shaving Rooms'. Penny haircuts were the mode until the Wycombe Hairdressers Association announced increased charges in 1915 for 'Shaving 1½d., Haircutting 3d. and an extra 1d. if the beard was trimmed. Children 2d. and 3d. after midday on Saturday.' This at a time when a local store advertised full furnishing for three rooms, delivered, for £5, and positions for servants were £10-£12 per annum.

29. This view bears the postmark 1905. On the left is the Thorpe Brothers' tobacconists and beyond that the creeper-covered house of George Stratton and the Literary Institute which was given to the town in 1891 by Baron Rothschild. On the right is the little shop which Cyril Batchelor enlarged and which was later taken over by 'The Rich Mrs. Robinson'. Beyond it is the Cross Keys. More creeper, evidently very much in fashion, covers its sign, the emblem of St. Peter, with its subscript 'For Cyclists'. A notice over the door proclaims it 'the only Free House in the district – horses and carriages for hire, with or without driver.' At one time not only good cheer but also Justice was dispensed here, the Petty Sessions being held on the last Thursday in each month. The Court moved to the George and Dragon by 1880 and later to the Institute where it continued to be held until 1979 before merging with the Aylesbury Bench. By 1924 Dr. Cooper and Dr. Wills were in partnership at the now 'Old Cross Keys' and the old sign, recently re-discovered in the attics, adorns the High Street once again.

30. The south-east end of the High Street had some very fine residences and until 1926 only one of Bloss & Sons several shops (augmented by a mobile van which gave them a virtual monopoly for some years) brought 'trade' to it. In 1926-1927 'The Yews', first on the left, was converted to business premises and new shops erected in its garden. Its neighbour, converted later, preserves its facade. In the distance the imposing house of Miss Philps was placed on a protected list of properties of outstanding architectural or historical interest in 1947, to be altered only with the consent of the Secretary of State. This consent was given seven years later, when the house was demolished together with the old White Hart and replaced by the London Co-operative Society Shops. Beyond it is Chester's bakery, with a glimpse of the fields where the houses of Hawthorn Road stand now.

31. The name of Jacobs had been associated with the mechanical needs of the town for well over a hundred years when this photograph was taken in 1910. William Jacobs, blacksmith, of the Butts, died in 1830, and Jacobs, father and son, have already been mentioned in Back Lane. Another William Jacobs had kept the forge just up the High Street, but at this time the smith was Mr. Collins, seen here, arms akimbo, behind the car. The manufacture and sale of bicycles had been George Jacobs' main business, an important one providing the main means of transport then. He is seen here at the wheel of a 1904 3-cylinder Vauxhall with sons Harry in the back and Frank standing in front. A man of few words, he could be relied on to carry out all manner of useful repairs 'for a bob'.

32. The site of Collins' smithy can be identified today by the outline of the windows and door of the house, together with its mock beam ends under the roof, themselves a feature of many houses in the town. A charming description of it in Leonard Bull's book, 'A King's Highway' leaves little to be said here, but the picture is included because of its importance in the life of the town to young and old at the time. One did not have to travel far to find a forge; there were, for instance, six between **Great Kimble** and **Risborough station**, and we shall discuss their importance later, in considering the one at **Monks Risborough**.

HIGH STREET, PRINCES' RISBOROUGH, BUCKS.   TAUNT & Co. 875

33. Looking back down the High Street today, as compared with this view in 1889, one misses the White Hart with its horse trough, and Miss Philps' house. Part of the White Hart was converted into Morris' small family butcher's shop, and then in the Co-op development it disappeared together with the house, to be replaced by shops and flats. On the left of the street was the Omer Pasha, a beer house and later cafe, which Mr. Leonard Bull told me had been formerly called the Saracen's Head, until that name was taken to new premises in Station Road. Omer Pasha was in the news at the time as a colourful figure in the Crimean War and his name must have seemed an appropriate substitution. Just beyond is the bay front of the smithy, looking rather better kept than in the previous picture.

34. These three cottages stood at the corner of the High Street and Bell Street, next to Barley's Chemist shop. Barley's survived into the 1960's, but the cottages were pulled down in 1937, having been used in part as a shop for the bakery opposite beside the White Lion. As seen here the cottages present a motley appearance, but the original timber framing can be seen under the eaves on the right, filled in with brick but probably originally wattle and daub. Mr. Williams, one of the last inhabitants, who courted here the wife he had watched grow up 'over the road' in Horn's Lane, told me that when the cottages were demolished the massive beam which supported them all was worth more than all the rest of the property. The house behind was occupied by Mr. Keller, a stonemason and organist at St. Mary's Church. The site, having been abandoned for 47 years, should see a new Library on it in 1984, appropriately enough in a year made famous by a book!

White Leaf Cross

35. Hill View and Ivy Cottages, with the Cross behind them, formed an attractive backdrop to Horn's Lane and were a pair of solidly built mid-Victorian houses, albeit with outside sanitation. Sold in 1979 as 'worthy of refurbishment to create splendid little houses', that wish expressed by the auctioneers, Hamnett Raffety, was not fulfilled quite as expected, as they were rapidly demolished to be replaced by the small block of flats which preserve their memory as Ivyhill Court, and may, when the new road is complete, add their own attractiveness to the corner. Behind them lay the 'Burying Field', itself remembered as Berryfield Road. Its origins are shrouded in the mists of time, but it used to be said that victims of the Plague rest there.

36. The invention of the light high speed petrol motor by Daimler in 1884 led to the rapid development of the motor car. Newitt's garage stood in Back Lane, next to Hill View and Ivy Cottage, and continued in this business until 1929. It was well-known because of its association with the renowned hill climbing events which took place at Kop Hill, and the rather home-made looking car on the right may have been built for just such events. Mr. Newitt is standing just behind the tail of this car, and nearby is a 4½HP BSA motorcycle. Inside the garage lurks the ubiquitous Model T Ford. Mr. Newitt also had a bicycle shop in Duke Street, in what were then separate premises at the rear of Lloyds Bank, now incorporated into that building. After the family garage business closed, the garage itself was used by Lyons Tea as a warehouse, and as a Government food store during the Second World War. Finally it was used to store construction machinery until it was pulled down with the cottages which had been Mr. Newitt's home.

37. During the 1914-1918 War the Government established a Central Tractor Pool for Buckinghamshire farmers, and Newitt's yard in Horn's Lane (with the garage in the background) was commandeered for the purpose. Farmers left short of labour could apply for one of these splendid machines and a driver to help with the ploughing and harvest and a Model T Ford was used to deliver petrol to the farms from a 40 gallon drum. Just as the garage and cottages have gone, so the yard has now been levelled to make way for the new road, having itself been the base from which Newitt's carried out much of the Public contractual work in the district.

38. This was the view from Copthill Road, now New Road Hill, looking down to the three landmarks of the town, the old spire, malthouse and brewery. The identity of the driver of the trap is unknown, but a Mr. Eggleton farmed at Brimmers and Major King lived at Wardrobes and there was little else in this direction. The ricks stand in Hays End Furlong, enclosed by what looks like a deer fence, so strong and high. Behind the hedge on the right was Money Dell's Piece, crossed by Love's Path, and all these fields remained unchanged until after the Second World War. Back Lane struggled to preserve its name and character until this year, but is now lost, a sacrifice needed to safeguard the heart of the town.

39. Cop Hill takes its name from Risborough Cop which stands on the right of the road and was also known as Soldier's Mount, having been reputedly a Roman hillpost. Coins of the Emperor Constantine and other artefacts of the third and fourth century A.D. have been found there. Cop is an Old English word meaning a top or head and the present spelling of 'Kop' may date to the presence of German prisoners of war, being used locally by 1920 but not officially until much later. Cop Hill was the scene of memorable hill climbs and trials for motorcycles and cars, held regularly until 1925, and at which speeds of up to 76 m.p.h. were recorded. Such events were common on the public roads, but increasing traffic was making them hazardous. It was probably less that than the lack of a Public address system which led to the two accidents in 1925 which brought matters to a head. T.R. Allchin crashed his motorcycle at the top right hand bend, and in the afternoon a Bugatti injured four spectators, and the R.A.C. withdrew all licences forthwith. Kop Hill Farm and House now stand on the left of the road and the little rise in the middle distance has been quarried away.

40. Leonard Pauling was an eminent photographer who emigrated from Longwick to New Zealand in 1903, taking with him a rare collection of pictures of the area. This is one of his studies, harvest time at Mr. Eggleton's Brimmers Farm. The latter half of the nineteenth century saw the introduction of mechanisation to Buckinghamshire farming, the first recorded innovation being a steam plough in 1857. The elevator, with Mr. Owen Redrup at its foot, is being worked by 'Horse gear tackle'. The thatched ricks are characteristic and might be of sheaves or loose, especially in a bad summer if the wind had laid the corn. Long straw wheat was commonly grown, and might stand over four feet high, but could be cut above the weeds and still be easily handled. A good man with a sickle could cut and bind a quarter of an acre a day or in the same time thatch a rick like these, a skilled and essential art in the days when Dutch barns, functional but less attractive, were scarce.

41. The boys are gathered outside Dorsett's Grocery and the imposing gateway of the Baptist Church. The name of Dorsett figures prominently in local history and is one of those mentioned in the 'charter' of Elizabeth I. The business continued into the 1950's when it was taken over by a succession of 'supermarkets'. We can think fondly of the boys with their hoops and cycles; would we look as kindly on them today? In fact the local constable had as much trouble with fireworks in the street and vanishing signs, not to mention litter, as occupy us today. With the trees on the left, the White Lion at its best, and Horn's Lane beyond, this corner of the town is a good example of rural Buckinghamshire. It used to be known as 'Duck End' and maybe there was a pond here, providing a local home for the Aylesbury Duck industry which, as we shall see, thrived at Askett.

Princes Risborough Bucks. Baptist Church.   Taunt & Co. 2975

42. The Baptist congregation acquired land for their meeting house in 1707, when the purchasers were described as 'Peculiar' more usually referred to as Particular Baptists, followers of Calvin. The original building was small, and several private houses were also used for worship. In 1805 and in 1814 the building was enlarged, at which time the pews ceased to be privately owned. This enlarged building is the one we see today, though surrounded when this picture was taken by fields on three sides. The Church has had several stormy moments in its history, the last referred to earlier when the 'Free Baptists' separated, but the congregation maintained a basic loyalty to the home ground, aptly expressed in a letter to the Inclosure Commissioners when a footpath was to be closed and members from Loosley Row entreated that 'the path to the Sepulchre of our fathers be continued as used by us and our forefathers from time immemorial for attending a place of Public Worship.'

High Street & Bell Street, Princes Risboro' from the Air.

43. This part of the town has changed a great deal since this aerial view of 1926. In the centre are the buildings of Ayres' Farm, and there and in the adjoining rectangle building is now in progress. The remainder of the open land is almost entirely covered already. The faint, straight track running diagonally across the bottom left corner, is the present Park Street. Behind the Bell and Bailey's Grocery is a long-since vanished thatched cottage, and the fourth building in the group is a pair of cottages, Jasmine and Lilac, belonging to George Jacobs. Jasmine Crescent and Jacob's Meadow now occupy all this area, and all the houses fronting the road from here to the tall house, now Raffety Buckland's offices in the High Street, have vanished. More than once in this book the loss of the old open spaces has been bemoaned. That is not to say that the land was freely open to all, but it provided a sense of freedom which is hard to find now, for all the care taken in the design of new developments. Time cannot stand still, but in an ideal expanding universe space should remain in proportion to growth.

44. On the right of Bell Street Thomas Bailey's grocery, like Dorsett's, was noted for its home-cured bacon. Public Houses called The Bell frequently commemorate the site where the Church Bells were cast, it being easier to bring the bellfounder to the church than transport the bells, and it would be pleasant to think that the peal of five bells hung in 1552 might have been made here. The thatched cottages on the left date from that time or in part even earlier; they are now converted into one house. Sandwiched between the two thatched roofs one can see the characteristic alteration in pitch when thatch is replaced by slate or tile and taller sash windows replace the older casements in the eaves. The cart just beyond the lamp-post is outside Mr. Benyon the wheelwright's, and beyond that the old 'Torch of Youth' road sign warns of the recently built Bell Street Schools.

45. This was how Henry Taunt saw the Wycombe Road and Bell Street in 1890. Children walking home from the British School in Parkfield would have passed only the Rectory, where Icknield Court is now, and on the left a new town house, Parkhurst, now called Park Meadow, and the Wesleyan Chapel built in 1869. The village pound used to be just up on the left, and the footpath, which is now Park Street, ran from just in front of the chestnut tree where the Post Office is today. On the right of the road were Nursery gardens, formerly a field called Pound Piece, and here the new schools were built.

46. Another 'bird's eye view', this time looking over Bell Street from the footpath which still winds up to Clifford Road and across what was called Shephern Hill to Culverton or left to Pyrtle Spring (the Purtwell) and Loosley Row. The 'new' schools had been opened recently and across the road the Wesleyan Church had acquired neighbouring houses. The parkland beyond the school was just on the market for development. This picture gives a good idea of how the old town concentrated on the right really did consist of 'one main street'. The schools, opening with 118 pupils, expanded to meet the growing needs of the town, and eventually covered much of this hillside with classrooms and playing fields before being closed in 1982 because of falling attendance rolls and the cost of rebuilding. The future of the site is still uncertain, but housing seems most likely.

47. *It is May Day. Rise up, and like the lark ascending, be strong, be glad, be thankful and be free.* So wrote J.H.B. Peel, echoing the feelings of all good country folk. These children from the Bell Street schools are in their finery for the Maypole dance. May Day dancing was a tradition carried on until quite recently and not only by the children. From the early hours groups of dancers would meet in the Market Square and wend their way up the High Street to the tune of fiddle or pipe. Tom Redrup, on the left of this picture, and his schoolmates, had a more complicated task, weaving the garlands onto and off the pole. The children of Longwick actively preserve the May Day traditions for us. The Bell Street schools were so called because they were strictly a Boys and a Girls School, and were the first of the new era of Local Authority schools, providing free education for all. Previously such education had been almost entirely the responsibility of charitable institutions, supported by Government grants and fees. The town had two main schools before this, as we shall see, and some small private schools, such as that in the High Street where in 1881 Eliza Locke was Governess and Martha Locke schoolmistress to seven boarding pupils.

48. The Wesleyan Methodist Church, like the Baptist Church, has a long history in the town which has always been strongly independent. The original meeting place was in Back Lane, at the rear of the George and Dragon, and can be seen in the aerial view of the town centre as a square building with a triple roof, just to the right of the brewery chimney. During the Second World War it was the headquarters of the Home Guard, having long since been given up as a place of worship. The new church was founded in 1869 and preserved its uncompromising but nevertheless imposing facade until the mid-1970's when the building was extended forwards to provide a lobby. The new plain facade, with its softly illuminated Cross, is somehow gentler and more comforting than its predecessor.

The Vicarage, Princes Risborough. 107958

49. The Old Rectory, as it was known in its latter years, was a very imposing Victorian presence midway between the 'town' and Parkfield, standing in extensive grounds with stabling at the rear, and housed at the 1881 census the Rector, his wife and three daughters, cook, servant and a student. It was eventually demolished to make way for the valuable Local Authority development of Icknield Court for the elderly, three Nurses' houses and Merton House for children. The latter recalls the long association of Merton College as landowner in the town. Just beyond the Vicarage or Rectory were allotments of the Agricultural Association, founded in 1860, on which the houses of Culverton Hill were built. Mention should be made in passing of the strength of this Agricultural Association, which counted Prime Ministers amongst its patrons, and whose Annual Show attracted national interest.

50. The junction of Wycombe Road and Station Road with the British School in 1900. The curve of the Wycombe Road was built as part of general improvement to the old Turnpike at the time of the Inclosures and was placed on the bank above the old road as 'the best means of avoiding the deep recess which the road makes at this point.' As much argument was heard as has been heard recently about the new relief road, including the possibility of bringing the new road straight over Shephern Hill, but eventually it was agreed that the line should run 'along a sweep within thirty yards of the Barroway', almost the only reference to this ancient track that I have come across. Just up the road from the school is Parkfield Cottage where John Pope Fordham, Inspector of Public Nuisances, lived with his wife and seven children, twelve years between eldest and youngest.

51. The British School was established in 1836, though the building dates from 1847, when it was erected by subscription at a cost of £450. In 1880 the average attendance was about 120, but when this picture was taken only 64 were present including May Redrup, later Mrs. Frank Spittles. The children all look healthy and well-clothed, but it should be remembered that at this same time the Headmaster of Wycombe Central Boys School found it necessary to appeal in a local paper for boots and shoes for his barefoot pupils — 'every recipient will present himself daily to ensure your gifts are not pawned.' The Baptists were the prime movers in the foundation of the school and it was used for a time as a Meeting House before the Iron Chapel was acquired, and also for social functions. In January, 1907, Miss Walker of Longwick received a postcard inviting her to a concert there — 'Won't you come if weather permits? There is a moon, you know.'

52. In 1920 the cinema came to Princes Risborough. With the opening of the new schools the British School was taken over, first as an assembly workshop for Goodearl's furniture and then managed as the Prince's Cinema by Mr. & Mrs. Wright. A projection room and lobby were added and inside was seating for about a hundred people – good solid Wycombe chairs in rows of six up the centre and two either side. A grand piano and full set of percussion were at the ready to create the proper atmosphere, and on this particular day the billboard on the right advertises Buster Keaton in 'Speak Easily' while over the door the names of Laurel and Hardy were a permanent enticement. Amongst the audience were often to be found members of the London University Officer Training Corps, come to camp at Kimble and apt to disturb the peace on their way home. On occasion the cinema doubled as a roller skating rink, more entertainment than the town can boast today. It was subsequently replaced by the rather grander Carlton, owned by the Boulting Brothers, which continued into the sixties, where Carlton Court is now.

53. This was Station Road in 1910. It used to be the main road out of Risborough, but by 1820 the sharp angle at the foot of Poppy Road had become too dangerous to be negotiated safely. An amusing letter to the Commissioners offers to take off their hands 'the triangular plot of little use' to be left between the new and old road; someone had a good eye for business. On the left with the man and cart outside, is the Saracen's Head, mentioned earlier in connection with the Omer Pasha, and where Frederick Clanfield retailed beer. Its yard now has a house fitted neatly sideways-on. On the right the hedge hides Long Park and the Salt Marshes, then open fields but now built over. It is not clear how the name Salt Marshes arose; there were certainly springs in the area, more particularly on the far side of the present Manor Park Avenue, but no evidence to connect them with salt, nor the famous 'salt boiler of Droitwich' mentioned in Domesday.

54. This chalk and flint cottage still stands today, the last survivor of a bygone era, tucked away so as almost seeming to be part of the ground on which it stands. This end of town was called Sheepbridge, perhaps in connection with an old drove road, though the old road did not turn right here down the hill until 'modern' times, continuing instead down Picts Lane as far as the mill where it crossed the stream and doubling back to Summerleys Road, thus avoiding the relatively steep climb the road takes now. The junction is popularly known as Friday's corner, after the butcher's shop which was next to the cottage but is now given over, amongst other things and curiously enough, to the sale of salt! Summerleys Road, in passing, was formerly known as West Eye Road, and a field called Wren Eye nearby hints at Saxon origins.

Culverton Mill, Princes Risboro'

55. Down Picts Lane stood Culverton Mill which by 1920, in common with all the local mills, was run by Mr. Silsby. It had an eighteen foot diameter wheel, but by 1923 the tail stream had silted up so much that it bore back on the wheel, making working very difficult. Silting and plant growth created problems in the headwater as well, as not only the miller but also the local swimming club found to their cost. The mill disappeared about twenty years ago, but part of the pond remains. It is interesting to note that Pyrtle Spring was the main source of water for this and Parkmill, and contributed to Longwick Mill as well, when today it is hard put to maintain any flow for much of the year.

56. Princes Risborough Swimming Club, as the shield which was rediscovered by chance in a second-hand shop near Witney testifies, was active from 1906 until the Great War. Included in this group are many important figures in the town, led by Major Coningsby Disraeli with his wife in front of him in the fashionable hat. Major Disraeli was nephew and heir to Benjamin Disraeli, and eventually moved from Horsenden Manor to Hughenden, but never lost touch with his friends in the town. On Mrs. Disraeli's left is Bill Chester, assistant chemist at Ridley's and baker. Next to him is Mr. Dyer, headmaster of the British School, and then Mr. Arthur 'Spider' Lacey, so-called because of his tendency to hoard useful things against a rainy day. Mr. & Mrs. Lacey were my neighbours for many years and his practicality was often in evidence. On the Major's right is Joe Dorsett, the grocer, and on the extreme right is Mr. Chalfont of the Buckingham Arms. The club used Longwick Millpond and held regular annual galas, negotiating a right of way across the fields. Attempts to revive the club after the war failed because both Longwick and Culverton ponds had silted to such an extent as to make them unusable.

57. The railway came to Risborough in the 1860's, after much bargaining, and the famous engineer, Brunel, was associated with its beginnings. The original station building, pictured here in one of Taunt's 'Shilling series', stood further along the platform than today's, opposite the Railway Tavern. The Tavern was a large boarded building with ample stabling, and John Dover ran it and the station coalyard, while Henry Mason was Station Master. Originally there was only a single line with a crossover for Thame and Aylesbury, but eventually the station expanded to four lines with two bays for the Watlington and Aylesbury lines. The goods shed is in the background with its own siding. The railway contributed greatly to the expansion of the town, but declined again in the 1960's, a hundred years from its beginnings.

58. The old Black Prince, a Wycombe Brewery house, must have been a cosy place, with its bay windows and the shade of the tree, but was inadequate for the growing needs of the town, with visitors to such new establishments as the Forest Products Research Laboratory, opened in 1927. The inn stood on what is the forecourt of the building which replaced both it and the warehouse in 1933. Another vanished feature is the old signpost, or 'finger post', giving as clear directions as many modern signs, and attractive enough for the County Council to put its name in the circlet on the top.

hiteleaf Cross & Kop Hill, Princes Risboro'.   *From the Ai*

59. We have completed our journey through the town, and before glancing at some of the surrounding countryside let us take a last aerial look at Risborough. On the left the road from Monks Risborough runs in past open fields, and on the right the Upper Icknield Way winds across the lower slopes of the Chilterns with Kop Hill striking up to the ridge. The triangle of field below Kop Hill and to the right of the Icknield Way will be mentioned again, and is the old Windmill Field. Only the faint impression of a path running across 'First and Second Park' in front of the church marks the future Manor Park Avenue, though the poplars at the foot of the garden of Parkhurst are those which now tower over Park Meadow houses, their tops rivalling the spire. Where the Fairway is now was Long Park with the Salt Marshes below. In the foreground a cloud of steam marks the station in its heyday. Further back, on the right, is Culverton Mill. Behind the triangle of Princes Place, across the Wycombe Road, a small depression in the corner of the field is the site of a ragpit and later an Observer Corps field post.

60. Saunderton Mill stood in the Bledlow Road, opposite the Three Horseshoes, and was demolished in the 1920's. For most of its life it was a paper mill and worked in conjunction with Bledlow North Mill, where rags were prepared and then at Saunderton turned into 'Small Hand, Royal Hand and Elephant' paper. When this picture was taken it was owned and used as a corn mill by Mr. Silsby, together with Culverton, Park and Longwick mills. Miss Silsby stands by the door, Mr. Green and Mr. Redrup by the horses, and in the background, by the hedge, is Stratfold Read, one of the town's most prominent citizens, Chairman of the Magistrates, Alderman of Buckinghamshire County Council, and Vice-President of the Agricultural Association of which Mr. Stanley Baldwin was President in 1925. This spot has even older memories; just behind it, partially excavated in 1938 but once more buried under the soil, stood a Romano-British farmhouse, and the whole area has signs of extensive occupation.

61. The imposing centre of this building may not have been matched by the rest, for it was the Workhouse of the Wycombe Poor Law Union. The Inclosures of the eighteenth and nineteenth century to quote the Reverend Shepherd of Princes Risborough, 'cramped the hand of the industrious cottagers and brought many of them on the Parish' and the small local workhouses, such as that in Risborough, were inadequate to cope with the problem. This one, at Slough in Saunderton, replaced it, serving thirty-three parishes, an area of 147 square miles, and stood in 11 acres of garden, on the site which Ortho Pharmaceuticals occupy. It is difficult to imagine the terrible problems that followed enclosure, for all the benefits of 'efficiency', but the Reverend Shepherd knew that the poor needed a defender when he reminded the Commissioners of 'what is written in Proverbs 14:31 and 22:22-23.'

62. This is The Whip at Lacey Green, where Sara Floyd was licensee. Behind it is the windmill, active until about 1910, and recently carefully restored by the Chiltern Society. This mill came to Lacey Green in 1821 and was owned by Lord George Cavendish, an important landowner of the time. Across the valley on Bledlow Ridge a post-mill stood until about 1933. Princes Risborough had its own windmill until the mid-eighteenth century and it is shown in a drawing done for Browne Willis in 1742 and now in the Bodleian collection. It stood in the great field above Pyrtle Spring, south of the Icknield Way and called 'Old Windmill Field' by 1820, the term Windmill Hill being applied generally to the whole hill between town and Pyrtle Spring. A likely site would seem to be a little rise beside an ancient depression called 'Barber's Pits' where it would have overlooked Culverton Farm.

White Leaf Cross, Risborough Bucks.   Taunt & Co 1845

63. Peters Lane, in 1904, was a chalk road with no houses on its right and only Whiteleaf village on the left. The avenue of trees had not long been planted, providing shelter for Whiteleaf House. Attractive as they are in themselves, they now completely hide the Cross from sight as one looks at the same view today. The first edition Ordnance Survey map shows that originally Peters Lane only came up as far as Whiteleaf village, and as one came down from Green Hailey this road veered off to the right under the Cross, where traces are still visible. The Cross itself is much more enclosed today, of course, and perhaps the sheep that were frequently to be seen on this road contributed, aided and abetted by rabbits, to keeping down the scrub.

64. Except that the road is wider, by cutting into the bank, Whiteleaf has preserved much of its appearance of 1900. It is in less obvious ways that it has changed, in matters that we take for granted today, like the supply of water. The man carries two pails of water on his yoke, collected from Well Cottage, and this was usual, though most houses had some means of gathering rainwater for ordinary use. In fact, the author remembers as a boy in Rutland the trips to the village pump, and the rainwater sump under the kitchen floor, from which the day's supply had to be pumped as the first chore of the day. Whiteleaf obtained a mains water supply in 1926, when the 'Rural Districts Water Company' built a reservoir tank near the Golf Club, pumping the water from Monks Risborough.

Cadsden & White Leaf (Longdown Hill)

65. Upper Cadsden presents a very different appearance today compared with 1900, particularly in the complete obliteration of the open view of Longdown Hill by trees, so that now even the road is invisible. The two Tudor cottages have been preserved, the left hand one as Whiteleaf Golf Clubhouse, though from this viewpoint modern extensions conceal all but the roof, and the garden has disappeared under outbuildings and car park. Lettering on the end of the cottage invites the passer-by to 'Coffee, cup of tea, cocoa' commodities to be sought for long and hard by the modern traveller of the Ridgway Path. On the right Thorns Lane is a broad track. Now named only at the Whiteleaf village end, and only a narrow footpath, it used to be a busy track uniting Whiteleaf, Upper, Middle and Lower Cadsden where the Plough Inn awaits.

66. 'This is my grandfather, Job Poulton. He was a snob,' said Mr. Cyril Poulton. Change, as we see, affects not only places and things but also language, and what we know as a derogatory term was here applied to that most valuable member of the community, the shoemaker and cobbler. The snob, in his leather apron, surveys his back garden, typical of its kind, in Letterbox Lane, Askett, towards the end of his ninety years, one of ten children. He would be seen, sitting by his door with his work on his knee, held in place by a leather band passing over it and fitting snugly under his foot to leave both hands free. In those days long before tarmacadam roads, his was a craft to be appreciated, particularly by Mr. Eggleton of Green Hailey, who took size 13 shoes.

67. The local Aylesbury Duck industry was represented by Horace East's poultry farm at Askett, now Pygle House. Many people kept a few ducks – a postcard tells that 'Aunt Emma is sending three ducks to market and Uncle John eleven and a chicken', but Mr. East and his son had a large establishment, employing, amongst others, Mr. Cyril Poulton's mother, third lady from the right, to pluck the ducks (except for the wings). Duck breeding was always a risky business, and a man might lose all his stock overnight from infection, but the Aylesbury was a large bird, maturing early, and might fetch between 6s. and 10s. at Easter in London, at eight to ten weeks old.

68. The site of this cottage where Jimmy Arnott lived, lies just to the left of the main road from Aylesbury at Monks Risborough, and all that remains is the yew tree that once stood in a corner of its garden. The old turnpike road ran much closer to the village than today, from beyond the school, up the hill towards Princes Risborough, and the lay-by in front of the houses is all that remains from when the new road was built in 1927. From here into Princes Risborough it passed open fields on the right and only a handful of houses on the left. According to F.G. Parsons, even that road was comparatively young, the old road from Askett coming into Burton Lane past the church and green.

Nags Head Inn ↓   Monks-Risborough   The Butchery ↓

69. A closer look at the old main road at Monks Risborough shows Mr. Lacey at the gate of his butcher's shop. Through the archway was the slaughterhouse, and from there most of the district's meat was supplied. Mr. Lacey's brother in Risborough High Street has already been mentioned in this respect. The lime tree on the extreme left no longer survives. It was one of a pair which at a later date gave the name 'The Limes' to a cafe on the site. In the first of the next pair of cottages lived 'Skimmer' Clay, who shared his home with his own hand-made coffin, not trusting to those thought suitable for others. He seems to have acquired his nickname from his habit of walking the woods carrying a sea-shell with which to skim water from any convenient pool, and was reputed to walk Whiteleaf woods in his sleep. Next down the road was Mr. Cummings and his forge, and across Burton Lane the old Nag's Head, with a separate cottage on the corner.

70. At the corner of Burton Lane Mr. Cummings, the blacksmith, sharpens a billhook. Apart from his care of the horse, the manufacture and repair of every kind of mechanical device made the smith an important figure in every community, and many a small boy took delight in turning the great grindstone wheel and watching the sparks fly, before the days of emery and carborundum. A good many country 'grandfather' clocks started life in a smithy, and the recently restored weather vane of Monks Risborough church is thought to have been made in this one. Down Burton Lane was Eggleton's bakery, at first on the left, but later on the right of the road where in this picture the high door marks the granary. Bread was baked in an open-fired oven in the wall, the fire being removed and replaced by the dough once the required temperature was reached. At a later date Eggleton's achieved more than local fame when three daughters of the house were featured in a national newspaper as England's answer to the American Beauty. The family business closed in 1966.

71. This is the 1896 team photograph of Monks Risborough Cricket Club. On the extreme left is the umpire, Mr. Baldwin, a master wheelwright, and next to him is Jimmy Arnott, gardener at the Old Rectory. Mr. Eldridge holds the ball and next to him is Mr. Arnott's eldest son, who was killed in the Boer War and whose brother fell in the Great War. Messrs. Wainwright, Baldwin junior, F. Rogers and A. Paxton complete the back row. Reclining on the left is George Lacey, the High Street butcher, then Messrs. Ashby and Tattersall, Mr. Higgins the schoolmaster and Mr. Durling, landlord of the Bernard Arms, known otherwise as the 'Bear and Cross' or the 'Bear and Forbear' from the arms and motto of the Scrope Bernard family. He built the house next to Askett Garage, calling it Forbear House, but now known as Wyvern House.

72. Mr. Cyril Poulton and his wife have made available several of the illustrations in this book and his family have already figured in two of them, and rightly so for he is one of a long line, who has contributed greatly to the author's knowledge and love of this 'corner of leafy Bucks'. Mr. Poulton looks back on ninety years of change and as a boy lived with 'The snob' who himself looked back to the time of Waterloo! As a young man Cyril Poulton worked for Mr. East of Burton Lane, and is seen here driving a brougham in 1912, outside the Old Rectory in Mill Lane and in the best livery for the wedding of Mr. Chapman and Miss Hill at Monks Risborough Church.

73. The sixteenth century Dovecote and some of the trees are all that remain of this scene showing Place Farm in about 1895. Kings Oak Close now occupies most of the site, the picture being taken from the church, with Mill Lane on the right. A short drive ran from Mill Lane to the farm, and a farm track from the village green. At this time the Pauling family lived here, related to the Woosters, who farmed Rectory and Chestnut Farms before moving to Meadle. These farms employed some twenty men. Chestnut farm belonged to an 'absentee landlord', never seen by the tenants who paid him rent once a year. Place Farm passed to a Mr. Hitchcock and was sold for development in 1960. The Dovecote is mainly built from deep chalk, usually referred to as 'rag' and used for all manner of building, including roads, hence the number of ragpits in the area. It has 216 cotes and is unusual in that they are set directly under each other rather than alternately, and also for its arched doorway, also carved from 'rag'. Frost caused extensive damage to the building in the past, but vandalism, so out of keeping with a Dovecote of all places, has made the attempts of the Parish Council to preserve it even more difficult.

74. Just before the story closes let us look at two groups of people, whose lives touched this era in a particular way. First of all, the defenders of our heritage, the Home Guard of 1914-1918. Facing his men is Mr. H.E. Newitt, and next to him Dickie Jacobs and his father. Elegantly turned out in the light coat is Mr. Charlie Bloss. Third from the left in the middle row is Mr. Saw, the sweep, and then Henry Nottingham of Duke Street, who succeeded Captain Stratton in the Fire Brigade. Appropriately enough the men are gathered in Little Park, in a spot formerly known as Backgate Butts, where earlier generations had carried out their compulsory archery practice on Sunday mornings. The Great War was the overwhelming event of the period, touching the lives of every family in a way never before experienced. Eighty-seven men who gave their lives are remembered on the Rolls of Honour in Princes and Monks Risborough and no-one having heard such veterans as Sergeant Jack Cross, of Butlers Cross, recalling the nightmare of the Somme could fail to be moved by their courage.

75. And here is what this War was for — the hope of the future. These are the children of the Church of England or National School, the class of 1922. Slightly younger than the British School, this was founded in 1841, for 140 boys and girls. Miss Janes, who lent me the picture, sits in the centre of the front row, white socks neatly pulled up, and she and her classmates can surely be proud of the town they have kept for us, and which has inspired another of its sons, Leonard Bull, here fourth from the right in the back row, to write of it with affection.

76. Let us finish our walk down the road of history with this couple. The main road at Great Kimble wound down the hill past the 'Bear and Cross' and the church, passing in front of Church Cottages where Mrs. Rutland chats with a neighbour at her gate. Photographed by Samuel Payne in about 1895 the couple are, at a guess, 'travellers' and not local residents, unlike Mrs. Rutland whose family had lived in the village since at least the sixteenth century. In the background is the old rectory, built in 1859 and known as Great Kimble House since the new rectory was built in the 1930's. Pickade House is now between house and cottage, hiding the view to the right and the valley where formerly most of the village stood, in Great Kimble Warren. The new road, of course, runs to the left of the hedge, where in this picture a little five-barred gate leads out under the tree towards the church with its old high-pitched roof. 'Oh, peaceful England!'